Bulletproof Business

Protect Yourself Against the Competition

Ryan Stewman

Table of Contents

HARDCORE RESOURCES

Facebook
125,000 followers
Fan: https://www.facebook.com/HardcoreCloser/
Group: https://www.facebook.com/groups/salestalk/
Personal: https://www.facebook.com/realryanstewman

Twitter
10,000 followers
Personal: https://twitter.com/ryanstewman
Business: https://twitter.com/hardcorecloser

LinkedIn
6,000 followers
Personal: https://www.linkedin.com/in/ryanstewman
Business: http://www.linkedin.com/co/hardcorecloser

Instagram
20,000 followers
Personal: https://www.instagram.com/ryanstewman/
Business: https://www.instagram.com/hardcorecloser/

#43 Business Podcast on iTunes, 3,000 subscribers
https://itunes.apple.com/us/podcast/ the-hardcore-closer-podcast/id1098856846?mt=2

YouTube
1.5 million views
https://www.youtube.com/user/ryanstewman

Clyxo
www.Clyxo.com/Closer
Snapchat
ryanstewman

Skype
ryanstewman

Blog
400,000 Visitors Monthly
Sales Talk For Sales Pros
www.HardcoreCloser.com
Articles, Digital Products, Training Resources

Books

- *Bulletproof Business: Protect Yourself Against The Competition (2016)*
- *Kick Ass - Take Names, Emails and Phone Numbers (2015)*
- *Hardcore [c]loser,* **A Top Business Book of all time, Amazon (Best Seller)** *(2015)*

Foreword

Business is much more about who you are than what you do or what you have.

And the faster you move in business, the more 'who you are' becomes exposed. Whether your choices of what kind of business to be, or what kind of person to be have left you safe at any speed. Or whether your choices to move faster, to be more visible have only exposed the unresolved issues with your business.

The bigger and more impressive the structure you choose to build, the more critical the necessity for a powerful foundation.

Among sales-focused entrepreneurs, it is very easy to 'sell' around the weak foundation. The gift of being able to explain every liability as an asset can have us convince ourselves and even those around us that our business is safe on the backs of our sales talents alone. And that all of the foundations needed for 'other' businesses is just too complex for us.

So, we build. And it falls. And we build. And it falls.

In this book, Ryan takes on the importance of securing the safety and stability of your business, so that you can then focus on selling at maximum speed without worrying about the inevitable fall ever again.

He's lived out all of the stories in the book, so that nothing comes from speculation or 'ideas', but only from making mistakes and turning those mistakes around. And from taking the lessons learned from those mistakes and building his own Bulletproof Business that he can be proud of.

For all of us with a passion for sales that drives our success at lightning speed—this book can help us never to get struck by the lightning that we have created. But rather, to be fueled by it, and in turn to create a legacy that lasts and grows and reminds us of how great we are.

Pick up this book and read it from cover to cover like I did. Then use it as a mirror for the absolute lack of concern given by karma. As a reminder that our results are far more a result of our reactions and choices than they are of any outside force. And then use the sage advice that Ryan shares to recruit karma and create the 'luckiest' business around.

In business, you deserve whatever you design and build. So, go design a business and a life that you deserve.

-Kevin Nations

Introduction

This book tells the true, grimy, dirty, filthy details of businesses failed and businesses gone wrong. The only way I've ever learned anything is the hard way. When you're a massive action taker, who makes instant decisions, you're bound to make some bad ones. The thing about me, though, is I never let one bad decision give me the fear of making another. What happens, happens.

In this book, you'll read the stories of the mistakes I've made, the lessons learned from them and how you can avoid them. This book is the real deal. Nothing in here is fake. The journey I've gone, to get where I am, has sucked. I've been fucked over more times than I could fit into this book. I've never let a fuckin' keep me from keeping on, though.

I'm not one to sugarcoat anything and this book won't sugarcoat shit either. These scenarios have taught me more than any Ivy League college ever could. From stories of prison, to the streets, to the corporate world, I've conquered them all and fallen each time. You'll read all about it. I promise.

When I say, "I've seen some shit," this book backs that up. This is my third book. Book #1 was about my life. Book #2 was about my business systems. This book is about my business failures and how each failure only made me stronger. After reading this book, you may ask yourself *why in the fuck did he keep on working*? The answer is simple. I have almost everything I want now. The only thing missing is a billion dollars. Give me 15 years and I'll be there.

This book is not for those folks who have a weak stomach. It's not meant to scare you off, but to prepare you for the hard journey ahead. Sure, some of us are lucky enough to hit it out of the park the first time at bat. Most of us have to fuck up 100 times before we win once. This book is about my 100 losses and how they will never take away my current win.

When you read this book, make sure you pay attention to the subliminal lessons. Sure, each chapter has a failure and lesson, but within each lesson, there are hundreds of sub-lessons. I figure you're smart enough to get the context, but I think it's worth telling you to be aware now, before you dig in.

Learn from my fuck ups. Take these lessons and apply them to your life and business. Avoid making the same mistakes I made. In prison, we called people who do dumb shit "crash dummies." Consider me your business crash dummy. Also, prepare to laugh your ass off. This book is the wildest business book ever written.

-Ryan Stewman

Chapter 1

Shots Fired

I'll never forget that day. It was one of the worst days of my life, yet it came with one of the biggest lessons and revelations I could imagine.

At the time, I had this company called Lifestyle Connections. Basically, it was a lifestyle company, which connected real estate investors with properties and then managed those properties for them. I'd been running this business and managing 37 homes for about six months. We had made a significant amount of money. On this particular day, I'd arrived back in town from New Orleans and was headed to the office. On the way to the office, I stopped at the 7-Eleven in Frisco, Texas, to put gas in my truck. I had a 2003 Dodge 1500 Ram, four-door, silver with nice 22-inch rims. It was the whole shebang. I started to fill up, but the pump said, "See cashier inside." I thought maybe something happened. It was a busy time of the morning. Reluctantly, I put the cap back on the truck and headed inside to the store.

I patiently waited in line. The 7-Eleven was packed. There were people everywhere. Construction workers were grabbing snacks and getting lottery tickets. People in suits passed in and out, grabbing Red Bull and swiping their cards. I think it was the busiest I had seen a convenience store in my life, or maybe it just felt that way because of what was about to happen. When it was my turn in line, I said, "I'll take 50 dollars on pump 13 outside." The clerk swiped my card, and it said, "Denied." This time there was no reply for me to "See cashier" or "Please go inside." This time the answer was, "Sir, I can't help you." I had driven from New Orleans to Dallas. My gas tank was running on fumes. I didn't know what to do. I had no money. I had to go back to my ashtray. I grabbed $2.35 out of the ashtray, waited in line again, embarrassed that my credit card didn't work. I gave the cashier the $2.35, and hoped it would be enough gas to get me to my office.

When I arrived at the office on fumes, I was angry about the credit card situation. I stormed up to the building, only to find that my keys didn't work. I'd been locked out of my office. The landlord, who was sitting out front, said the rent wasn't paid. There was also a letter from my business partner, Bob. The letter said, "Don't bother trying to come to work today. I've taken everything away. I've discovered you're a fraud and that you've stolen all sorts of money. I've already alerted the authorities, our other business partner, Brent and everybody else who's involved. Fuck off."

I held the letter and began going over everything in my mind. I had been out of town. I hadn't caused any problems. I'd been doing the right thing. I was the one who actually ran the business. Bob didn't even know a thing about real estate. He was just the money behind the business. I realized what was going on. I was being set up. It was all being taken and scammed right in front of me. Within a couple of hours, I realized what exactly was going on. Bob had stolen my money and shut me out of the business. Before I could contact our other business partner and explain what Bob had done, Bob got to him and blamed it all on me, which made himself look better.

Now, I had to clean up the story. I got in touch with the other business partner, Brent. He agreed to meet me for lunch at a local restaurant. When we sat down at the restaurant, I could tell he was nervous, angry and very judgmental. I come from a pretty sketchy past, but I was also one of the smartest people running in our circle at the time. Maybe even the smartest one. Because of that, most people around me always thought I was one step ahead of them, that I was going to scam them. When people live in fear, they make irrational decisions, like Bob in this particular story. I sat down with Brent, and I told him my side of the story, explained what happened and why it had happened. I said I had just gotten back from New Orleans to find the credit card was turned off. To show him that I hadn't stolen any money, I shared the withdrawals from my bank account card, which was now locked, so we had no access. As I was proving to Brent my side of the story, I could tell he was still judging me with extreme skepticism. I wasn't just frustrated with the current business situation. Now, this guy who I had known my entire life, believed some bullshit business partner over me. It not only made me angry, it really hurt me. I realized I had made myself entirely too vulnerable. I had exposed myself and been too trusting. We didn't have the proper paperwork filled out. We didn't have an agreement on who would pay taxes. We didn't have any agreement that would have protected me from this situation. The money was in Bob's name. He felt like he owned it all. I could tell we were getting set up. Brent was too damn dumb to see what was about to happen.

That month, my house payment didn't get paid, obviously, because my assets were frozen. I had no way, no means and no education to run out and hustle up a few extra thousand bucks to pay my mortgage. So, shortly thereafter, I was faced with foreclosure because unfortunately, Bob owned the house, and he wouldn't pay the rent either. I had put my entire life and business in the hands of one man who was able to take it all within a matter of minutes.

Because Bob was the landlord, and we weren't able to afford the rent payment now, he went down to the courthouse and had us evicted immediately. With just three days' notice, I had to move down the street to one of my parents' homes. Actually, I had to buy a house from my parents to be able to move into it. Bob had taken all my cash, and my entire business model. Then he disappeared, poof, into thin air. I was left exposed, wide open and vulnerable.

To make matters even worse, he talked to the FBI and told them I was manufacturing methamphetamine, which was not true whatsoever. He knew with my sordid past it would be a believable story, since I lived in nice homes and had nice things. So, the local police began investigating me, too. My life had turned into a nightmare. I was anything but bulletproof in life and anything but bulletproof in business.

That lesson and that story that I've just shared with you will set the pace for the rest of this book. It's going to get a lot worse before the lesson is learned. Then it gets a lot better.

Chapter 2

Twist the Knife

Before the fiasco of becoming suddenly homeless, having to quickly buy a home from my parents and having no money for mortgage or a car payment, I had made plans. I was going to take a family vacation with my grandparents, my birth father and my brothers and sisters. I hadn't spent a lot of time with them, so I was looking forward to it. This vacation had been paid for back in October, and it was March at the time. Seemed like perfect timing. With all that I had been going through, I could go on a cruise and relax for a week. Since I was going through hell, I figured why not go on the cruise. The only sad thing about the cruise was that I couldn't afford any booze because I had zero money. I didn't want my family to know. I was too proud to let them in on the fact that I was going through any sort of struggles. Plus, I didn't want to be the guy who had gone to prison, who now didn't have any money, and would mooch off the family. I'm above that.

Anyway, I went on this cruise for seven days. On the way back home from the cruise, I stopped by a mortgage company in Dallas who owed me a paycheck from a closing I had done previously. The paycheck was exactly $3,200. I was overdrawn in my bank account by $2,200, and I needed all the cash, so I stopped by a check cashing place and cashed it, even though I paid God-knows-what in fees. I put the cash in an envelope and stashed it on the top of my visor, then drove home to Allen, Texas, a sleepy, bedroom community north of Dallas. About 45 minutes later, I finally arrived in my neighborhood of Twin Creeks, with $3,200 cash money tucked in my visor.

When I pulled up to my house, I saw cop cars, SWAT teams and ambulances. I had no idea what could have happened while I'd been gone for a week. I thought maybe something had gone down with my roommate and my business partner, Brent. He was the sketchy guy who hadn't believed a word when I'd told him Bob had stolen my money.

But when I hopped out of my truck, I heard, "Get him!" The cops came at me full tilt and tackled me and punched my girlfriend. Then they threw us both in handcuffs. I still wasn't sure what was going on at that point. I thought maybe somebody had hurt Brent, and they thought I had something to do with it. I also thought maybe they were there because Bob had sent them and it had to do with mortgage fraud.

They were there because of Bob, but it had nothing to do with mortgage fraud. They were looking for methamphetamine. The problem for them was there was no methamphetamine in the house. I hadn't done any drugs. That wasn't my thing. I wasn't into that. I was a house flipper, an investor making a decent living. Because of my past and a sketchy character named Bob, I found myself in a vulnerable situation again. Within a matter of seven days, this guy had taken my business away, taken my house away and now he was fucking with my life. I didn't know what in the world I was going to do.

They didn't find any methamphetamine. However, they did find a Glock .45 caliber with a 17-round clip. They took the gun, charged me with felony possession of a firearm, and stuck me in jail with a $25,000 bond. I paid the bond to get out. The bail was $2,500. As I left jail, I wondered what the hell I was going to do with my life.

This raid had taken place at three o'clock in the afternoon. Kids were getting off the bus and neighbors stood at the edge of the street. Cops were everywhere. They threw a flash bomb inside my house, even though Brent swore the front door had been unlocked. This was an over-abuse of power to make me look terrible. It had all been for nothing. When they didn't find drugs, they had to pin something on me, so they chose the gun. Technically, the gun belonged to my parents who had moved out of the house just eight days before in a rush, to move into another house so I'd have a place to live.

Now, I'm out of jail and I'm trying to get my life together and figure out what's going on.

I'm at a place in my life where I literally want to shoot myself. I am facing jail time again with a serious charge. I'm homeless and labeled a drug dealer. The neighbors can't stand me. I didn't know what to do. So, I reached out to an old hard-money lender friend of mine, Rob. I asked Rob if he had a flip house I could possibly move into for a few months while they were working on it. I told him I'd be willing to do whatever it took. It turned out Rob had just gone through a divorce and had an extra house that he used to live in about three miles down the road from the house that had just been raided.

I got Rob to agree to rent me the house for $1,200. I don't know what I did to come up with the $1,200. Maybe that was all that was left of the $3,200 I'd gotten in Dallas, after paying my bail to get out of jail. It took eight truckloads, one at a time, to move me, with the help of a friend named Chuck Branch and my girlfriend Stephanie. At the end of the day, we'd gone from a beautiful 4,100-square-foot house with a saltwater pool out back, to a 1,400-square-foot house on a corner lot in an old part of town.

At least, I was free. I was out where I could handle my own business and do something. But I had to start over from scratch. I wasn't sure what I was going to do, how I was going to do it, or who I was going to do it with. The problem was I had left myself too exposed. I'd put all my trust, efforts, earnings, and money into an account with these other two business partners who weren't the people I had thought they were.

Eventually, Bob's mother would end up suing me to get even more money out of the situation and get her homes paid off for free. Believe it or not, she would actually accomplish her goal. We'll learn about that in the next chapter.

You're not going to believe the story.

Chapter 3

Losing It All, For Real This Time

Wouldn't you know, as soon as I move into this house, my ex-roommate, Brent, tells Bob exactly where I live. Bob got my address, and his mother, Carlotta, sent me a summons letting me know I was being sued. Supposedly, she forged her husband's signature on some documents. However, an attorney at the title company witnessed and notarized her forging the document. Since she was guilty of forgery, she decided to point the finger first, which made her somehow exempt from conviction. I was being charged with possession of a gun that wasn't even mine in a house I didn't own, for a crime I hadn't committed. Meanwhile, this bitch had stolen houses, forged signatures, gotten a notary to lie for her and turned around and sued everyone. She sued me based on some cockamamie story her son, Bob had told her. It was crazy to sit there and read 17 pages of attorney jargon about how I had committed fraud and done the wrong thing. The papers said that even though she had forged signatures, she had done it because we had encouraged her to do it. I hadn't even been present at her closing. The title company, Richmond Title, was so big back then, due to the AmeriQuest meltdown, they had cameras everywhere. I was clearly not there that day intimidating anybody. But that wasn't what Carlotta screamed.

Once again, my sordid past had come back to haunt me. I found myself in a position where nobody ever believed me because I'd made a mistake when I was nineteen. You see, when I was 19, I tried cocaine one time. I overdosed. The person I was with called 911. Responders came to the house. After they revived me with a shocker, they turned around and charged me with manufacturing and delivering cocaine. I ended up having to do two years in state penitentiaries even though it was my first offense. I was a small-time drug dealer. I was given no choice. Because of that checkered past, every time something happens, I've always been the person to get the blame. I've always been the first one they look at, the first one they investigate and the last one they believe. I hadn't quite learned that lesson yet at this point in my life. I was still asking myself why these things always happened to me, but I was beginning to see why. I was an easy target because of my past.

Because I wasn't there that day and I didn't know the entire story, I did some research into Carlotta's story. It turned out the title company had notarized the notary book and filled out all the information stating that Carlotta's husband had signed on the title of the homes, even though he had not. Texas is a community property state, which means if you have a house and you're married, whether it's an investment house or a house of primary residence, you have to put your spouse's name on it. In this case, Carlotta was purchasing the house, but her husband, for whatever reason, was not aware of what she was doing, so she signed behind his back. That alone tells you what kind of a sketchy person this was that I was doing business with in the first place. Some guy named Kerry, who happened to be an attorney, worked for the title company and had notarized her husband's signature even though he hadn't been present at the time. Carlotta had obviously swiped his driver's license or something like that.

Six months after buying the homes, she received notices that because she never made a single payment on the homes, they were going into foreclose. She turned around and sued us as if she thought that she would get these homes absolutely free, no payment needed.

I kid you not. She sued the title company even though she forged the documents. On top of forging the documents and suing the title company, she sued us because we didn't make her payments. This lady fully expected never to have to make a payment on these properties and that she would own them, mortgage-free. Maybe her son had told her this, but I definitely had not. It is the title attorney's job to sit there and explain the whole documentation process, what her mortgage payment was, who her bank was and everything else. This lady literally, somehow pulled the wool over everybody's eyes but mine. All it did was make me mad.

When it finally came down to it, they subpoenaed me into her attorney's office. I refused to pay for an attorney, mainly because I didn't have any money. The only money I had that I could use to pay for a lawyer was going toward the gun charges that I was facing within the state of Texas. I surely couldn't afford to fight two battles at once. I had to pick the one that would take my life away, versus the one that would just financially crush me. I showed up at the deposition to defend myself without an attorney. I went on record, video, book, everything else, consistently telling them, "Fuck you. Suck my dick. She's a fucking cunt. We didn't do this. We didn't do that. It's all bullshit."

I was real and I was raw with everybody in there. No fucks given. Six weeks later, the judge dropped the case against me. He said if I'd pay a dollar for the court costs, one dollar for the court costs, then he would drop the case against me. After watching a video of me saying, "Fuck you. Fuck this. We didn't do this," he saw the conviction in my eyes and finally took my side.

Thank God, I hadn't spent all my money on an attorney to defend myself. They would have drawn that thing out forever. However, things weren't so lucky for the title company. Even though she'd forged signatures, the fact that they'd notarized the documents and did what they did, put them in a position where they had to settle and give her $1.2 million in cash. Ultimately, they had to shut down the entire operation, and lay off over 180 employees. It was crazy. They lost their E&O license. They lost their ability to write title insurance. I'm pretty sure the attorney who signed the notary box, as a favor, ended up losing his license and everything else, too.

Now, within a matter of two months, I saw two businesses I had thought were thriving, awesome businesses, get completely shot up, and left to dust. I knew I had to shut it all down. I had to build something that was stronger than that. I had to stop trusting other people. But that's exactly what I did again. I trusted someone else.

Wait till you hear the next chapter story.

Chapter 4

Employee of the Month

Even though, in the past, I had left my life in the hands of another business partner, this time I decided to leave my life in the hands of a corporation. I went to work for a private mortgage bank. Working at that bank was awesome. I actually had a friend named Mike who was a partner in the bank and their top producer. He took me under his wing and taught me what I needed to know about how the operations worked, how to make money, how to do FHA loans and the process followed in that company. He taught me how to write my own checks, and helped me to build a successful mortgage business. I was closing anywhere from 15 to 30 deals every single month, while working there. I worked my way all the way up to become that guy: the employee of the month.

The operations manager liked me. I had built a pipeline. I had a lot of investors. My loans were salable. The clients loved working with me. Everything was going perfect. I thought I had finally put everything behind me. I started earning serious paychecks again. I started living a decent life. I was paying my rent to the hard-money guy with no questions asked. We were actually enjoying living there. Everything was going smooth. I'd even gotten my girlfriend a job as a junior processor for Mike, in order to help him out with cheap labor, and for her to learn the mortgage business at the same time. In the event that I went away to prison, she could take over my business.

The massive pipeline I'd built had a lot of loans. I had this connection out in Los Angeles with these guys who ran a Century 21 on Beverly Drive, or maybe it was Wilshire Drive. They had this awesome Century 21 office anyway. They would send me a bunch of people who were selling houses in one part or another of Compton. They were buying First Texas, which was, and still is, a huge builder down here in Texas, so they were buying houses left and right and I was doing the loans for them.

I had reached out to Richard, the owner of Century 21 in Los Angeles and Beverly Hills, and had a conversation with him via phone. He actually flew out and met me in person. I was writing, at this point, 16 to 17 deals every single month, ranging from $250,000 to $350,000, for these investors who all had ace credit, who all paid money down. It was a dream come true of a mortgage pipeline.

I got so focused on these investors that I learned every single thing I could about investing. I built a massive connection out in Los Angeles, for people who were transplanting from California to Texas. I built a massive connection of builders who would give me rock-bottom prices in order to do volume, because at the time, mortgage lines of credit were getting harder and harder to procure. They were trying to free up as much as they had on their lines. I was scooping them up left and right and hooking investors up left and right, too.

I was everybody's hero. Things were going awesome on top of the repeat and referral business I was getting anyway. I thought I had made it to the pinnacle of the mortgage business. I was doing three, four million dollars a month. Nobody in the game was doing it like me. Right out of the gate, six months into it, I had found a honey hole. I was proud. What nobody knew was, the second day on that job, I had gotten a phone call from the ATF. The previous month, before I'd taken the job, I'd gone to court and gotten the handgun charge dismissed. My lawyer had beat the charge for me. I thought everything was perfect, but after dropping the charges, they had turned my case over to the ATF.

It was a completely different story with the Feds because you don't beat the Feds. They had a shoddy case. They were worried that if they lost the case I'd come back and sue them, which I would have. So, I got a phone call the second day I was at the office. I never told anybody except for my parents and my girlfriend. They were the only people who knew about the whole incident. I kept it all to myself. I had built this huge business at the mortgage company, with nobody knowing my secret. Before long, it was getting worse. It was getting closer and closer. I could feel the heat. The ATF were calling me on a regular basis. They were checking.

I remember one day, I had closed 30 loans the previous month, and the operations manager came downstairs and said, "You know, the ATF just had a conversation with me. If you weren't doing a whole bunch of loans, we probably wouldn't even be talking right now." I remember that feeling, like, *shit*! *I'm in somebody else's hands again. I'm not in control.* Not only was the ATF controlling my future, just like Bob could have destroyed it, I had an operations manager, an HR person and a Harold breathing down my neck, waiting for me to slip up.

It was frustrating, so frustrating. I felt, once again, vulnerable, like these people didn't like me. They *didn't* trust me. As I said in an earlier chapter, I was always the person under suspicion. Any time something went wrong, people always thought it was me.

They always blamed me. I was the first one they checked into when a crime was committed, whether I'd done it or not. Just like you see in the movies, that shit was real with me.

Chapter 5

You're Fired

Let's go back to that phone call that I'd gotten on my second day on the job. The ATF asked me to meet them at the bank. These are the same people who burnt down the Waco building, the Branch Davidians stuff. Because I'm from Texas, the ATF is a scary name with a huge stigma attached to it. They were in charge of alcohol, tobacco and firearms. I had a gun.

The special agent, or detective, dick, whatever they're called with the ATF, reached out and said he wanted to talk to me about a gun I'd had back in 1999. When I'd gotten into trouble originally, I'd had a gun in my possession, because, after all, it's Texas. Everybody has guns here. That's just normal. In the commission of a crime, they act like everybody's a damn gunslinger or whatever, whether you have a gun for hunting or not.

They had questions for me. I was going to go down there and straighten it up. Little did I know, when I arrived at this building, they'd meet me down on the first floor right outside the elevator. They knew exactly what I looked like, what I drove and had me on camera pulling up. They slapped handcuffs on me in front of everybody. At that point, I halfway thought it was some sort of joke. I'd gotten a new job; somebody called me to meet them at another bank. I was hoping it was some sort of gag. Everyone would laugh, and I'd get a release by punching someone's face in for wasting my time. That wasn't the case. I wasn't punching anything because my hands were handcuffed behind my back. The ATF told me, "Get in." I got in the car. They changed my handcuffs from behind my back to in my lap. They put me in the front seat of the car. The other detective rode in the back. They recorded everything with a video and audio recorder as we drove from Plano, Texas to Sherman, Texas, which is about 50 minutes with no traffic.

On the ride, they asked me a series of questions. I gave them honest answers because truthfully, I had no idea why the hell they were there. I hadn't committed any crimes. I hadn't done anything differently. The story is what it is. What they're trying to do is see if I know any gun dealers. They're trying to get me to snitch on people who are at gun shows and things like that. I was scared to death. There's no way I'm going to snitch on a gun dealer. Those guys will shoot you! I explained to them that I didn't know any criminals. I told them I've lived a good life, look at my record, and so on and so forth. They drove me all the way to the federal holding facility in Sherman, Texas; checked me in and immediately had a probation officer come in and drug test me.

Lucky for me, I was at a period of my life where I wasn't smoking marijuana. I was just handling and minding my own business. For whatever reason, I wasn't doing any drugs or anything like that. That wasn't my thing. I peed and took the urinalysis. It was clean as a whistle. They then said because I'd passed my drug test I could go home, that they'd put me on pretrial release. The next morning, that's exactly what happened. They let me go. I had to meet a judge. My lawyer showed up. My girlfriend showed up. I met this judge via video conference who told me what I was on probation for, what my charges were and what the expectations and outcome for my situation were likely to be. Once again, I was vulnerable.

I had to go back to the office, (where I would later become employee of the month like I talked about in the previous chapter) and explain to them where I'd been on my second day on the job. I told them I'd been in real estate meetings all day. I'm not one to lie, but drastic times call for drastic measures in my opinion. This was one of them. I needed my job. It was what forced me to hustle my butt off to build the pipeline of investors from California who were moving to Texas; to serve them at the highest level and do as many loans as I could because it was my last chance. I was going to have to spend a lot of time and money on lawyers.

The lawyer I hired was an interesting story. He ended up later becoming the district attorney of Dallas County, not to mention, the first black district attorney and elected official in a county position seat of his nature, as well as the first Democrat elected to be district attorney of Dallas, Texas. Needless to say, it was a unique time in Dallas politics when a man, who had run a $300 ad campaign won, versus a guy with a $300,000 ad campaign. My attorney, a black Democrat, was the underdog, the one who was never expected to win. But he crushed the polls, beating out the white dude with a lot of money, who was a Republican—the typical winner in the state of Texas—especially in Dallas. My lawyer shocked everybody.

I was there with him along the way. I helped him market. I helped him refinance his house, so he could pay some more money for his campaigns and so on and so forth. He told me he would go to work for me and negotiate to make things happen. About the time he had been elected district attorney, a group called the Scarecrow Bandits had pulled a series of bank robberies. Down the road, the Scarecrow Bandits would be captured by the Dallas County Sheriff's Office while doing a neighborhood sting. That attorney, Craig Watkins, would later use the Scarecrow Bandits as bargaining chips to get me an offer from the ATF. I'm no attorney and don't know how the legal stuff or the legal system works inside and out, but he somehow used this group of robbers.

The original offer was for 25 years. After the Scarecrow Bandits were apprehended, my offer dropped to 15 months. 15 more months! I had already done 24 months from late 2000 into early 2002. I was not ready to go back. Nobody ever wants to go back to prison, especially for something they didn't do. The ATF wasn't hearing it. The federal system, for those of you who don't know, has a 97 percent conviction rate. Nobody fights the Feds and wins. When they make you an offer, if you don't take it and you go to court, chances are they're going to make you do 10x your sentence. I'm all about 10x-ing life and 10x-ing commission, but I didn't want to 10x my time inside. I settled for the 15 months and did what I had to do. They gave me 60 days to get my affairs in order.

Within that 60 days, I had to make some drastic, irrational decisions because my life was about to go into someone else's hands again. I'd transferred my life and my business from Bob to the banking industry. But I'd ultimately lost that job despite the amount of production I put out. I wouldn't say I was fired, but I was encouraged not to come back.

Now, I was about to put my life in the hands of a woman. I was about to be vulnerable once again. You'd think I'd have learned to take the reins of my own life. The mistakes that I'm telling you and sharing with you in this book are to compel you to not make the same ones I've made. They're to learn from my mistakes.

Plus, who are we kidding? They're both interesting-as-hell stories to read. Would you rather read a business mechanics book that would bore you, or do you want to read about what happens next to ol' Stewman, your pal here?

By the way, if you're not a subscriber on my website yet, www.hardcorecloser.com, you should be. You're going to love it over there. Go ahead and sign up. Get a copy of my other book while you're there, too. Make sure you sign up and grab my emails. Then make sure you check your spam filter because sometimes they wind up in there. You're going to love that website. Again, check out www.hardcorecloser.com.

Chapter 6

Female Betrayal

Within those 60 days, I had to make some pretty quick decisions on who was going to run my affairs. I had a stock portfolio with about $50,000 in it; I had a pipeline with about $250,000 worth of commissions and I had about $25,000 in cash saved up in my bank account from the few months that I had been top producer over at the mortgage company. Plus, my girlfriend at the time, who was living with me, had downgraded from a brand new car into a used Altima. We still had really cheap $1,300 monthly rent and she was saving her paychecks from my buddy, Mike, too. I had accumulated, at a young age, quite a bit of money laying around at my disposal, based on my corporate job. I hadn't gone on any more vacations. I hadn't blown any cash. I had done everything I could to protect myself.

Like most young men, I was convinced I was in love. I was sure I was going to prison, but I was convinced my girlfriend would stick around. We flew to Vegas and got married by an Elvis impersonator. Believe it or not. I bought her a thousand-dollar ring. We spent the night at Caesar's Palace, had a great time and then came home. I put her in charge of my stock portfolios, my bank account, my pipeline and everything else. I positioned her to be successful for 15 months to where she didn't have to go without. She wouldn't have to deal with, or worry about anything. Worst case scenario, if she screwed it all up, there was enough cash in the bank account to get her through the next 15 months. All she had to do was put a hundred dollars a month on my books, pay my truck payment and everything else was pretty much covered.

I was supposed to turn myself in on June 15, 2007. On June 12th, my stepfather was having a birthday. We had dinner at Steve Fields in Plano. As I've stated before, I hadn't smoked marijuana in quite a while. After we'd had a couple of drinks and steak dinners, knowing that I was only two days away from spending the next 15 months in prison, I asked my then-wife if she could call her brother, who was a drug dealer and a loser, to see if he could get some marijuana sent to my house. When I called him, he asked us drive to his place but didn't want to drive to us. I explained that I didn't want to get pulled over with weed and that I just needed this one favor. I had loaned this guy money before. I had done favors for him. I had let him crash at my house. He pretty much never paid me back, never did me any favors and now he wanted me to drive to him just because he was stoned and lazy.

As soon as I hung up the phone, I started yelling about how much of a fucking loser he was and how ungrateful her family was for some of the things I had done for them. She took extreme offense to that, which was probably offense-worthy, and said she was taking me to my parents' house. As I've mentioned earlier, I had some ownership stake in my parents' house. She was convinced that I could just go there and stay there. But that was their house, where they lived. It was my dad's birthday. For all I knew, he was probably about to bang my mom. So, I didn't want to deal with all that. I told her I was not going to my parents' house, that she could go to her parents' house if that's what she wanted to do, but we were married and had a four-bedroom house. She was more than welcome to sleep wherever the hell she wanted. She busted a U-turn, insisted on driving down the street and taking me to my parents' house. I waited until we reached a red light and she started to slow down. From the center console, I put the car into neutral. I started pulling the emergency brake up with one hand and turning the wheel with the other. I guided the car into the parking lot of an abandoned business on Bethany Drive in Allen, Texas. As soon I pulled the car to a complete stop, she got out and took off walking. I immediately hopped over into the driver's seat and put the car back into drive. Then I pulled up beside her, rolled the window down and asked if she'd like a ride home. She got in the car after a couple of minutes of convincing. As soon as we got to the light and I put the blinker on to make a left and took my eyes off her, she reared back and punched me as hard as any man's ever punched me in my life, including prison. My eye instantly blacked out, swelled up and my face started bleeding. Then, she reached back and hit me one more time. My other eye swelled up. I thought my nose was broken. I grabbed her hand to ensure that she wouldn't hit me again, but she started jerking around, so that she could get free and hit me again.

I'm flying down the street at this point going 90 miles an hour in a 40 mile per hour zone. I got to the house and ran inside to the bedroom and locked the door. Ironically, I put on a wife-beater t-shirt, a pair of Adidas pants and just sat alone in the dark corner of the closet with my head between my legs. I guess she called 911. The cops arrived and talked to her. They charged me with interference with a 911 phone call— however, they managed to get that to stick. They also charged me with family violence. On February 12, 2007, the Allen Police Department arrested me even though I was the one who had taken the abuse. I was the one who had taken the punches. All I had done was defend myself while operating a vehicle completely sober.

I didn't realize it at the time, but much like Bob, Stephanie had a plan to set me up. A month before, when she'd found out I was going away, she couldn't stand the fact that I was leaving. So, she started dating the guy who was doing my landscaping when I wasn't around. When I had to go to Sherman, they would go out on dates. When I had to go to a business meeting and tighten things up, they'd meet at the house. I had no clue all of this was going on and that I was being set up.

That night, while I was in jail in the Allen Police Department, once again for a crime I hadn't committed, she was freezing my assets, getting power of attorney filed, (that had been already drawn up weeks in advance) getting restraining orders and packing my stuff. She was setting everything up so she and the gardener would be able to live happily ever after on my production pipeline, my assets and everything else I had made while I was in prison. I couldn't do anything about it, because there was no way, once she put the restraining order on me, that I could liquidate those accounts in just 24 hours before I had to go to federal prison.

My life had been put in the wrong hands of somebody again. I had gotten married for the wrong reasons. She left me for the gardener a few weeks after we had gotten married. After doing a few months on the inside, I got a letter from her saying she was divorcing me. I didn't know at the time; it was for the gardener. She said she was divorcing me for somebody she had met two weeks before I'd gone to prison, that the whole thing was a setup, and if I ever tried to do anything about it before I got out, she'd burn all my shit, and I'd come out with nothing.

I was the most vulnerable I'd ever been, again in the hands of somebody who I thought loved me. I had a lot of thinking to do over the next 15 months. And I was kind of thankful to be in a bubble where I could get clear with my thoughts by myself and figure out how in the hell I was going to align myself to where I wouldn't be that vulnerable in the hands of anybody else ever again.

Chapter 7

The Big Release

Out of the 15-month sentence, I ended up doing 13 and a half of them inside a federal prison that didn't have air conditioning during one of the wettest, most humid seasons ever in the history of me being alive in Texas. The judge had shown mercy enough to only send me 45 miles away from the city I lived in, which was nice at first when people would come visit me. After I got the letter from my wife telling me she was divorcing me and warning me that she would be burning my shit, I just wanted to be left alone. I wanted to be left alone with my own thoughts, with my own time to think things out. I sought several religions, read the *Bible* cover to cover four times; I read the *Koran* and the *Torah*. I did everything I could to start finding myself. I read *The Art of War* and *Atlas Shrugged*. I wanted to gain knowledge.

Every time I'd found myself in vulnerable situations, where people ruined my life, I'd allowed it to happen, simply because I was uneducated. I hadn't graduated high school. I'd spent time in prison. All I'd ever known was washing cars and doing mortgages. I had consistently gotten in trouble. I had crossed the line every time I was doing mortgages. It was a frustrating process. The reason I'd partnered up with other people was because I was insecure. I thought I had shortcomings. I thought those things meant that I didn't have experience. I thought those things meant I couldn't become an expert.

I learned from each experience, maybe not fast enough, but I became better and better. Each time I read a book of other people's experiences, particularly entrepreneurs, I realized other people made mistakes, too. That's what made them so great at what they did. I realized guys like Steve Jobs, Rockefeller, and other guys that had done all these successful things and created all these awesome inventions and legacies, had struggled and gone through some of the very same problems I had. Some of them had even spent time in jail. I got my mind set right, and nothing mattered other than the fact that I had the experience. I had gone through the experiences to get the expertise, to be able to go out there and call myself an expert. I could explore the world in a way that nobody had explored it before. I would be able to be bold and confident, and I would understand because I had read 500 books while I was locked up. I had been put through the process and had a real understanding of how the world worked. I understood the laws of attraction from a religious standpoint, and so much more. I had the proper mindset that when the time arrived to go to the halfway house, I could stay there and get focused on re-adjusting to the outside world.

When I was finally released in July of 2008, I went to a halfway house in the southern part of Dallas. One day I found a magazine sitting there that talked about living in high rises in certain parts of town. I'd always lived the suburban life and thought that was the coolest thing ever. I remember the first day the halfway house gave me a bus pass to go out and look for a job. I went to the place where that magazine had advertised and laid eyes on a brand-new tower called the Azure. The Azure was amazing. They wouldn't even let me inside. I probably had the most terrible clothes and smelled like the halfway house, too. I told myself, one day I'm going to live somewhere like this.

I wasn't really searching for a job. I was only going to be at the halfway house for two weeks. So, I took the train north to go visit my parents for the first time in I don't know how long, to say hello to them. I realized there was a new development going up across the street from North Park mall. I went in and took a look. They showed me some of the upper floors and penthouses and I was hooked. I told myself that one day I would live in that location, and I would live my life on my terms.

After spending two weeks at the halfway house, sitting around, reading the last little bits of a book, gathering the last bits of knowledge, listening to the guys that did have jobs talk about their struggles, it was time for me to go home. The sad part was that going home wasn't as fun as I thought it was going to be. You see, most of my friends didn't have jobs anymore. Most of them weren't even in the mortgage business anymore.

If you'll recall, in 2007, as soon as I was locked up, the economy and mortgage industry collapsed. It fell mainly because of the House committee, and because Congress changed over from being Republican-ran to Democratic-ran. The mortgage market melted. Money leaked everywhere. Many of my friends' banks had closed down. They went out of business. They had to collect benefits. Many of them were getting charged with mortgage fraud for things they hadn't done. Meanwhile, I was locked inside a bubble the whole time. When I got out, most of my connections to get back into the mortgage business didn't work in the mortgage business anymore. Many of them had already left, cursing the industry. Some of them had committed suicide.

I was going home to nothing and without any chance in the mortgage business, I didn't have a chance at anything. I was going to live with two people that I could barely stand—my parents. I know, I know, everybody has beef with their parents and stuff, but I just felt way disconnected from them. They'd always given me a weird vibe. I just never really liked being around them. Much like with the detectives and everybody else, when I was around my parents, I always felt they thought I was the one who'd caused them grief, that I was the one who put them in certain situations. Anytime something happened, say, liquor went missing, even though it might have been my sister who drank the whole thing, they always blamed me. It was just an odd feeling and I hated it. I felt almost more comfortable living with another cellmate in Seagoville than I did going home. At least I knew if I hustled my ass off, I could get the hell out of my parents' house sooner than later.

Chapter 8

The Big Talk

I asked my parents not to come and pick me up from the halfway house. I rode the DART Rail from Westmoreland, instead, which is far south of Dallas, to Parker Station, which is where the train ends in the far north. I wanted that whole train ride to make a transition, as I left that part of the city in Dallas County where the prison happened to be, and traveled up north, back to where I lived. I wanted it to be like an emergence, as if I'd come out of the tunnel at Cityplace and wound up on the north side of Dallas as a new person.

With big hopes and big expectations, I didn't know some of my friends were dead and most of them unemployed. I didn't know the mortgage business had gotten that bad. I didn't know a lot of people weren't as strong and bulletproof as I'd thought. I didn't know yet that many of them were facing charges. I had huge, exuberant expectations for what could happen for the second and newest chapter of my life.

My stepdad came to the train station to pick me up. He was perfectly on time. When I got in the car, he said, "Before we do anything, we need to have a talk." He went on, "This is the second time you've put us through this, that you've gone to prison. We're going to invite you to our home, but here's the deal. There will not be a third time. It's not that we don't love you. It's not that we don't trust you. It's that we won't deal with this ever again. You've put yourself in this situation." He talked on and on and on. All I could think about was two things: one, at least I was free; and two, I wanted to punch him right square in his face, because it was his gun that was in that house. The son of a bitch was a convicted felon as well, and he should have manned up and said that it was his gun and not mine. Instead, he said nothing, and I'd gone to prison for it. Whether it was my business partner or not that led to the cops kicking in that door, my stepdad had a felony, and he still held the gun despite his felony. He's the one who had caused this. All I could think was, *that was your gun and I ended up doing the time, because you're stupid. I didn't ask for that gun in the first place.*

Here he was telling me that I needed to get my shit together. Meanwhile, I'm the one who helped them buy the house they were living in.

At this point, (but I didn't know it yet), they were months behind on their mortgage payment and their marriage was in shambles. When I got home, I found out some terrible things from my sister. It was all I could take. I just wanted to get out of there. I wanted nothing to do with them ever again. I wanted to escape.

I met back up with the girl who I originally had broken up with when I was 19 years old through social media. I just wanted to do something and get out of there. She had a house in Wylie. I ended up moving in with her in a very short period of time. We rekindled a decade-old relationship after two stints in prison. I cleaned up my life. I started going to church. I started doing the right thing.

People came at me with jobs. There were very few real options, because folks had mostly left the mortgage business. They were selling me some kind of crap. I tried to help these people called the United Cities, who were buying up houses with fake deeds. Once I found out what they were doing, I left. In no way, did I want to enter the fraudulent mortgage market, because for many of my friends, that was not going too well for them.

I worked for another insurance company helping recruit life insurance reps. It was boring work and something I didn't believe in, like selling rocks in the cemetery. I was just not interested in it whatsoever, despite the opportunity to make money. I didn't like to learn the lingo. I didn't really care that much because it was a really boring job.

These were the type of options that kept coming my way; very few and very limited. When I moved in with Ashley and I started living there, I changed everything up. I decided I was going to go full speed and return to a job in the mortgage business, even if everybody else was failing there. I decided that something was going to happen to me and something was going to put me in a position to where I could go get that job at the mortgage bank. I set my sights on going to work for the top privately owned mortgage bank in the state of Texas. And that's exactly who I went after.

Chapter 9

Scavengers

Once I was released from prison, I bounced around from job to job. It was like everybody tried to offer me something to do. People wanted me to sell everything from life insurance, to some sort of property scam. People offered me off-the-wall weird titled jobs saving foreclosures. Scavenger after scavenger threw jobs at me. They all pounced on me because they assumed since I had just come out of prison, I was going to be needy, and this was their chance to exploit me and take advantage of me. After being vulnerable so many times, I realized I had to keep my eyes open for the scavengers. They were just like people inside of prison, trying to take advantage of me because I had commissary money and I did my own time. It was the same way when I got on the outside.

I did work for a couple of them at first. Obviously, I'd gotten burned a few times. Like I never got paid. People used to tell me,

"You should take advantage of this opportunity, this is the only one you've got. You're a felon. This is your last chance."

Then they wouldn't pay me.

After weeks and weeks of going through the same process over and over, I finally talked to my girlfriend and explained what I was going through. I was like, "Man, I need some help. I need some clarity. I need to know what I need to do. What do you think I should do?" Then I had to have a long talk with myself and get my thoughts together and really understand what it was I wanted.

I felt so burdened by the mortgage industry because the job I had going in wasn't available when I got out. While I was gone, I had turned over my entire pipeline to my ex-wife. She had not only made it to where I couldn't go back to the bank where I had been a top producer before, she had given me a bad name. They had already known I was going to prison and promised me my job back, but because of what happened that night before I went in, and she had told them all sorts of stories—I wasn't around to defend myself…so, I was pretty much black balled at that bank. Completely burned. I had put my life once again in the hands of somebody else.

But I realized that when I'd had the corporate job at the bank, I had built a pipeline. I had lived a good, clean life. The job had kept me in line. It had been kind of like being on probation. When I had a corporate job, they made me show up at a certain time at a certain place, kept me on point and kept me producing. I am so competitive that when I show up at a corporate job, I want to beat everybody else around me.

Meanwhile, the jobs the scavengers kept offering left and right basically involved me competing against myself. I didn't know what to expect, because nobody else had gotten any results. After a long talk of trying to get my life together and everything else, I decided I was going to go corporate. I was going to go to work for the top bank, the largest independent, privately owned mortgage bank in the entire state of Texas. I put my sights on them.

Then I went through my network until I found somebody. My buddy Mike, a different Mike than the one at the original bank, had switched over and started working for another company and he said he could get me an interview, but that was as far as he could go. He would make a recommendation. He wouldn't mention my checkered past. All that would be up to me. I had one shot, one opportunity to get in front of the owner of that company and have a conversation with him. I wasn't going to let that conversation go to waste.

In the next chapter, I'll explain exactly what I did, exactly what I said, how I played, how I begged, how I ended up back in a corporate job...and my actions from that point on.

Chapter 10

Top Producer...Again

A couple of days before I was to go interview for the top mortgage bank in Texas, I had a flat tire on my truck. I was completely broke. Each tire on those 22" rims cost somewhere around three-hundred bucks. I had zero money. I couldn't afford the tires. I put the spare on, and I drove the truck to a used car lot. Right then and there, with only $4,000 or $5,000 left owed on my truck that was, at least, worth $10,000, I took a $7,000 tab, rolled it over into a 2003 Infiniti G35 so that I looked more like a banker. It had four tires. Now I was rolling from a nice truck to a used sports car.

I showed up two days later in my used sports car to TexasLending.com, the largest privately owned mortgage bank in the State of Texas at the time. TexasLending.com had 60 loan officers, five teams, a huge HR corporate closing processing department and they were a machine spending roughly $150,000 a month in advertisements on TV and radio. They were a well-known brand in that area that was sometimes respected, but sometimes hated.

I knew if I could get in there and get the job, and they provided me with leads and one opportunity, I would be able to make the top producer position within a matter of 60 days. I knew I would help everybody in the company get to a whole new level because I was so competitive. I finally walked into that interview with Rob Beesley and I begged and pleaded. I told him my felony didn't matter. I showed him my W2s from before I had gone to federal prison. I told him if he just gave me this one shot, I would not let him down. My license was still active. I was still hungry. I still remembered how to do loans. I still knew how to get on the phone. Prison hadn't changed me. I was hungrier than ever. I would do whatever, and I would not let him down. That meeting lasted almost two hours. Rob drilled me, and gave me every objection known to man. I stayed fast, and closed over every single one of them to the point where he finally said, "Mr. Stewman, I want to take a risk on you that I've never taken before. We're going to send you down to get drug tested. If you pass the drug test, then we'll give you a shot here. If you make one infraction, then we will be more than happy to escort you to the door. We don't want any problems here. Is that 100 percent understood?"

I closed the boss. I had explained to him my situation. He had given me every objection possible, but I'd closed over every last one. Now my job was to pass this drug test, then prove to him he had made the right decision. I drove down to the drug test lab of their choice the next day, took a nice piss in the cup, handed it to the cute nurse and walked out. A week later, I started training along with three other loan officers. We had to go through three days of training to learn their system, how they operated and all that fun stuff. When we were all turned into our cubicles at the end of it, I remember two of them going, "Dude, we got a lot of leads to call. This sucks." But I sat down, thinking, *man, I've got a lot of leads to call. This is awesome."*

That day, I had two applications. The next day, I had four. Within a week, I had 10 applications working in my pipeline, which automatically put me ahead of everybody else on the team. Within 90 days, I was making more money than 99 percent of the company. Other teams might have closed more loans than me, but I was a one-man army. I closed more loans by myself than anybody else in that entire organization. The boss would consistently walk by my cubicle on the way to his corner office, and tell me I was still a good decision, that he was glad he'd taken a chance on me.

Within 90 days, I was the top producer across the board in the entire company. I negotiated raises for other loans officers. I ended up building my own team. I had a 63-year old assistant, who I turned into a closing machine. When I first met him, he couldn't do anything other than print out emails. By the time I'd left the company a few years later, he would be the assistant to the CEO, and he is still the assistant to the CEO. At the time, Bob and I had built a team as I'd conquered the mortgage industry.

In 2009, when the mortgage meltdown was happening, people were going out of business and shutting their doors. Even though it was the end of the mortgage world, I managed to close 183 loans. And I felt pretty good about that.

Then 2010 rolled around. Because of our good old federal government, once again I found myself in a situation. The Dodd-Frank Act passed. Because of that, and because of my felony, or crime of moral turpitude, such as selling, manufacturing and delivering cocaine, they took my license away from me. They wouldn't allow me to operate and sale loans anymore. My whole world was over within a blink of an eye. It had all disappeared again. Everything I had worked for since 2008 until 2010 was gone in an instant.

I'd been diligently saving money, so I had about $30,000 in my bank account. I'd been paying my girlfriend's bills at the time. We had an upcoming wedding and everything was falling apart. With nowhere else to go, no license and no job, the scavengers had returned in my life.

It was a very, very low point. Within a few days and over a few months, I'd find something that would give me a spark, but it would be hard to ignite it until several years later.

Chapter 11

Homeless and Hungry

A few months into it, I decided to get my game together. I tried multi-level marketing, and made a few dollars. I did some odds and ends jobs to pay the bills and make things work. I never really found any kind of solid foundation to land on, though. I bounced around from this opportunity to that, maybe making a few dollars off this scavenger or that scavenger, but nothing ever really worked out for me. There came a point when, after my girlfriend and I were married, she found out she was pregnant.

It was a good time. I was excited. However, I didn't have my life financially together, which happens to a lot of people when they're not ready to have kids. I had to figure things out quickly. I enjoyed sales so much. I enjoyed working for corporations so much. I knew I couldn't make money in mortgages anymore. I knew I couldn't get a real estate license, so I went and I sold cars for a while. I had a friend who I had met in federal prison who gave me an opportunity, because he was the general manager of a car dealership and had worked his way up from the bottom. He wanted to see me do the same. I immediately went to work, and sold a car on my first day. He said he knew that he had made the right decision.

I continued to work there 70, 80 hours a week selling 25 to 30 cars every single month, becoming top producer, until it just wore me out. With a kid on the way, and a pregnant wife at home, with my schedule and living 45 miles from the place where I worked, not only did I show up at 8:00 in the morning, I had to leave at 6:30 to get there due to traffic; I was stretched. At night, the dealership closed at nine. It would be 9:45 or 10:00 before I got home. I did this six days a week, with Sunday as my only day off. It was an exhausting business. I loved getting face-to-face with people, helping them find their dream car and watching them drive off; the excitement of dropping the top down and explaining how the technology works and everything else, and I sold a lot of cars. But then my son arrived on September 9, 2011, and I knew I didn't want to work 80 hours anymore. I wanted to be home with him. It was time to build my own bulletproof business. I was going to have to make my own rules. I had a son who relied on me. I needed the insurance. I needed the money. I couldn't go rogue. I had to take a chance.

We rented out our house in Wylie and moved in with my in-laws. They lived in a nice house in Plano, Texas, where there was plenty of room for us all. It allowed us to save our money. I went to work creating my own business. When you live with your in-laws, as you can imagine, it can be a stressful time. Everybody is on edge, no matter what size the house is. You're expected to do things you wouldn't normally do. You have to act a certain way and be a certain way. It was a frustrating time for me. I was trying to grow a business. I was trying to raise a kid. I was trying to be a husband. Now, I had to do that under the microscope of my in-laws. It was at that time that I started to realize I had made a mistake and that I didn't want to be married.

I wanted to be free and to roam. I wanted to be able to make my own rules and not have to answer to somebody else, but I was stuck in a place to where I wasn't able to do that. I was in a place where I was forced to perform. I had no choice. I had to make enough money to get myself out of the situation.

With the utmost respect for my wife and her family, we just didn't fit together. My personality and the way they live their lives just didn't match mine very well. That's OK. Nothing is wrong with any of them. I have a tremendous amount of respect for all of them. At the same time, I realized I was in a bad position and I had to get myself out of it if I was going to keep my sanity. I had to also figure out how in the world I was going to deal with all this. Where was I going to make money? Where would my next paycheck come from? I dabbled on the Internet a little bit. I didn't know a whole lot about making money online. I had sold some multi-level marketing products. Obviously, I had sold some cars through the Internet as well.

I knew I could create revenue through Facebook and some of the other social media sites. I wasn't exactly honed in like an expert on how to make money from this stuff until one day, an old friend of mine who used to be a real estate agent invited me to lunch. There, he told me he was printing money off the Internet, like he was walking around in the One-Horse Saloon blazing guns in the Wild, Wild West. When he put it in that manner, it caught my eye, and that's when I knew I had to get on the Internet.

Chapter 12

The Internet is Real

I'll never forget the day I showed up at the Genghis Grill in Frisco, Texas, and my boy Mike Reiss walked in with a red Keller Williams shirt and khaki pants. He said he'd been at the red Keller Williams event. I wasn't sure exactly what that meant, but Mike was boiling over with enthusiasm. If you know Mike Reiss, you know he's an enthusiastic guy anyway. To say that he's boiling over with enthusiasm means it was almost uncomfortable for me to be around him. He was so excited. He told me that since I'd been locked up, he'd gone out of the real-estate business, and started selling coaching and training to real estate agents, using the same processes that had allowed him to be the top producer in the county at the time.

Back in 2005, Mike Reiss and his team sold real estate, while I did the mortgages. We all worked together as a team. Basically, every time somebody needed to get a home loan, they would send them over to me as their top referral receiver. In the meantime, I would make sure, through my mortgage practices, that they would close on time. I took care of the team and the client as well. We made a good fit together. When Mike met me for lunch, he explained he had left the real estate business after making a lot, maybe over a million GCI a year. GCI, if you're not familiar, is gross commissions income. He had made all this money, yet was leaving to pursue a full-time life on the Internet. He went on to tell me about these guys named Ryan Deiss, Frank Kern, Mike Filsaime, Andy Jenkins and Preston Ely, who were all doing really cool things online at the time.

After we were done eating, and I had listened to Mike just unload, and verbally vomit all this cool stuff, I was intrigued. Mike was the best in the business, in the busiest county. He had made over seven figures a year in a business he loved. If he was making enough money from the Internet to allow him to leave the real estate industry, then he was onto something. I followed Mike out to his Hummer. He opened the back door, and said, "Here's this program. It's called Ryan Deiss' Continuity Blueprint. Follow this whole thing. Figure out how the Internet works, and then I'll talk to you a little bit more about it all."

I took the program home. On the way home, Mike had sent me a text saying that the program I had in my hand was worth $1,500. My mind was blown. I had never heard of, or invested $1,500 in anything, let alone just a set of DVDs that I was going to watch. I was, needless to say, super excited to see what $1,500 worth of value was like. When I got home, I popped it into my HP laptop. The DVD started playing and it was so simple to follow. It made so much sense on how to set up Internet web pages, and how sales would follow. I was immediately hooked. I'd never understood that it was just a series of pages and links to other pages, and buttons that you installed. I never knew how the Internet worked. Ryan Deiss explained it in that program. He showed me how everything he said was right. I saw how easy it was to make money online. He made it seem simple.

Being the action taker I am, I immediately got to work. I found another multi-level marketing product, started marketing online, and made a little bit of money here and there. Then the company I was working for changed the compensation plan on me, and screwed me out of some commissions in the long run. Again, I learned that I'd been vulnerable. I'd put myself in the hands of another company and it hadn't mattered whether it had been a corporation, a multi-level marketing company, or anything else. I realized I was repeating the same process and making the same mistakes over and over again. That's when I thought I'd try it on my own.

I went to bluehost.com, and registered a URL called prisonexposed.com. I made a PowerPoint slide show based on YouTube, following the Continuity Blueprint. I followed some videos on YouTube that taught me more and searched some of the gurus. I ended up making this video about what to expect when you go to prison. The video started off telling people that they could opt in, and find out everything they needed to know about the first 48 hours; from leaving the county, to entering the prison, whether it was federal, state, or whatever the expectation was. I deemed myself Breeze McMahon, a convict who had done both state and federal time, had seen the inside of more than thirteen prisons and had been on the yard of more than eight. I talked about my experiences, and described what everything was like.

I found that a bunch of women opted into it because they were concerned about what their husbands who were facing time would have to deal with. The product took off. I sold it for $9.99, and I ended up selling quite a few of them. I didn't get rich, but it gave me hopes and dreams that a living like this could exist. With no SEO skills and no money to pay for advertising, I managed to sell a few hundred books at nine dollars each, and a few hundred videos at nine dollars each.

I was pretty excited about the entire process. Then I found a way to advertise on Google PPC. As I invested a bunch of money. I thought, *well, I don't want the world to recognize my voice, and know that I'm the guy behind these prison stays*, because see, I was still hiding that fact. I was concerned about it. To forego that venture, I started a venture on how to make money processing loans in my special way. I targeted loan officers on Google. Well, that month through my targeting and my keywords, I earned about $30,000 which super excited me.

I was bouncing all over the place. Mike Reiss was right. Ryan Deiss was right. This Internet thing is real. It's amazing! I dumped all $30,000 in an attempt to double down into selling more products, and I did. Then another law was passed in the mortgage world and everything I had invested in changed. My world was swept up from under me in the form of refunds. Not only had I lost my advertising money, but now I had to refund the programs because they weren't applicable to the new law. Again, I was broke. I didn't know what to do. I didn't know how to do it. I was sure tired of riding this roller-coaster.

I have been up and I have been down. I have been up and down more times than a short person on a trampoline, who hit on the anti-gravity set on Mars. I had just had enough of everything. I wanted to bang my head against the wall, and never deal with any of this stuff again. But there's something inside of me that just won't let me lay it down like that. There's something inside of me that just won't let me quit. I knew this Internet thing was real. I had a taste. It was like winning a couple of hands at Blackjack. I knew it was possible to make money from gambling. I just had to figure out how to count the cards better.

I went back to the basement. I didn't cut my hair. I probably changed clothes once a week. I focused all my time and energy on learning the Internet, and figuring out where I'd messed up. I found an opportunity to start working for real-estate agents, and loan officers in the sphere of social media, and I created a company, this time by myself, but with two other partners. I'll tell you about it all in the next chapter.

Chapter 13

Postfuser

This time, I decided to go all in and run a business by myself. I had an office inside of a title company. Through that title company, I ended up connecting with a real estate agency right down the street. This real estate agency was a startup with a pretty innovative model and they wanted me to join their team. I was skeptical about putting my life in the hands of someone else again. So, I decided to go in as an independent contractor.

I switched offices from the title company to the real estate company. Each week, I gave training on social media to real estate agents. Social media back then wasn't necessarily a popular thing. People didn't believe in it like they do now. As a matter of fact, most corporations, businesses and employers had blocked Facebook and other social media sites like YouTube from their company computers so employees and salespeople didn't waste their time. It wasn't like I was welcomed with open arms, like today's social media managers are. This was an innovative, forward-thinking company willing to take a chance on me.

When I worked for the real estate company, I used it as a testing ground. I was making hardly any money, but I could figure out what worked, to encourage agents to do certain things I recommended. I wasn't a licensed real estate agent. I wasn't a licensed loan officer anymore. I needed somebody who could test my theories out. Someone who could take action with the ideas I had, so I could actually get the results I wanted and use them as a testimony to my brilliance in social media marketing. Through that company, I met a couple of other guys who were outside-of-the-box thinkers as well. One was Chris; the other one was a guy named Andre. They were both forward-thinking guys and liked what I had to talk about. They liked the energy I brought. They both offered to partner up with me and create a social media management company. We would start with recruiting all the agents to do business with us who worked inside the real estate office. We were literally right in the middle of the testing ground with a pool of prospects we could start pulling from immediately.

Back in those days, we decided we would charge a $500 set-up fee and $100 per month for us to post to Twitter, LinkedIn and Facebook, every single day, three times a day, for every agent willing to pay us. We built the company up to about 10 people. Chris was gay, and he reached out to his boyfriend and borrowed $50,000 seed money to run the company. Immediately, and with that $50,000, Chris and Andre decided we should all take $10,000 apiece. I was broke as fuck. I didn't have any money. I was going through a rough time. I agreed to take the $10,000.

If you think about it, $50,000 with $10,000 each to three people, that's $30,000. All we had left was 20 grand. We had taken more money in payment than we had invested into the company. Again, I wasn't a smart business person at this time. I didn't have

my act together. This was my second
attempt with business partners, and I wasn't
sure what to expect. Then the three of us
decided we would spend some of the
$20,000 on a flight to San Francisco to go
to an Inman conference. We wanted to rent
a booth in San Francisco, and pitch to agents
as they walked by. We would tell them that
for a $500 setup fee and $100 a month, they
would get their social media managed by
some of the best people in the business.

Chris decided to buy first-class plane tickets,
so that took a lot of the 20 thousand. We
stayed in some of the nicest hotels. Again, I
didn't have a choice; I just went with the
flow. That also used some of the money.
Then, when we got there, honestly, San
Francisco seemed like a better place to party
than to work. I hadn't traveled that much in
my lifetime. It was only the second time I'd
ever been to California. I didn't do a whole
lot of pitching. My business partners had
promised they had a pool of prospects they
could pull from and that we would get rich
overnight. I remember it as one of my first
experiences where people promised wealth.

I had to learn that anytime someone promises you wealth, it's not true.

Folks didn't believe in social media like they do these days, still we went out there and pitched. The sad thing was, the Inman conference wasn't mainly real estate agents. It was mainly vendors. There were absolutely more vendors than real estate agents, which meant there were more people trying to sell shit than buy shit. It was a really shitty situation. I decided to go check out the Golden Gate Bridge instead. Eventually, I flew home with my tail between my legs and not a single sale made. I promised I would never go back to another Inman conference. I've heard that still today, there are more vendors than agents who show up at these things. What a waste of time, money and effort.

As soon as I got home, I had a meeting with the guys about having to go to work. We'd blown all of our money and we needed to go back to work. Andre, like a bitch, quit. He said it wasn't in his best interest, that he needed to focus on his other job. In no way, shape, form, or fashion did he offer to give us back the ten grand. A couple of weeks later, Andre actually tried to sell us some stuff that we had already bought as if it were his own idea and invention. Man, you just never know with some people. That was my first serious encounter with somebody who was 100 percent bullshit. He probably still is.

It left me and gay Chris together to do our business. We went on the road a couple other places and made some sales. And eventually, we built up the company to 77 people. We had $7,700 coming in each month, plus the $500 we'd taken from each of them originally. The sad news was that we were writing 210 social media posts every single day, across three different channels. It was a pain in the ass and it took all day to get it done. Nowhere worth the $3,000 a month we were making. It was only a matter of time before I told Chris I had to follow my dream, do things on my own, and once I had, we worked separately.

Chris continued to run Postfuser on his own. Eventually he moved to Thailand and caught a drug addiction. He ran up a bunch of credit cards from people without their permission, and stole a bunch of money. Since then, Chris and I have made amends. As far as I know, he's apologized and paid back everybody he stole from. But the market had left a bad taste in my mouth. Obviously, because of my former working partnership with Chris, when he stole people's money, I was guilty by association. Like, I've told you in chapter after chapter in this book, people always suspect the felon when something goes wrong. It put me in a bad position in the marketplace. I didn't know what to do. I was stuck. I was on the hook, just as well as Andre and Chris, for the money that Chris had blown. Chris was nowhere to be found. He was off using stolen credit cards over in Thailand.

Once again, bullets had been fired, and once again, I'd been shot. I had been fucked over. It was all on me this time. I was tired of working with partners. I was tired of having my life ripped out from under me. I was tired of building something up, only to watch it fall like a Jenga block pulled from the bottom. I was sick and tired of working with mediocrity. I was sick and tired of having half-assed business partners. I was sick and tired of everyone relying on me to pull the weight and get the job done. I put my foot down.

When I put my foot down, I said I would never do anything again that I didn't 100 percent control. I stepped into a place of power. I will forever be grateful for the one main thing Chris taught me: how to be myself. Chris was flamboyant and gay as hell. He didn't care what people thought about him, how he dressed, or anything else. He taught me I could be me. I could cuss. I could say, "Fuck, shit, bitch." I could do the things I needed to do. I could get tattoos; I could be Ryan Stewman and still attract the talent I needed. I'll always be thankful for that lesson from him.

I'll never forget the pain I had to go through, until I finally decided to put my foot down.

Chapter 14

Break Free Academy

I was finally fed up with putting my life in the hands of business partners, corporations, women and everything else. I was tired of being broke. I was tired of riding the roller coaster going up and down, up and down. I was tired of reaching the pinnacle of success and then hitting rock bottom, then reaching the pinnacle of success and hitting rock bottom again. I put my foot down and I said, "I'm going to create an event that I run and have people come to, instead of doing the work for them." I learned with Postfuser that I did not want to write 210 posts every single day. I did gain the experience through writing for Postfuser to call myself an expert in social media, however. What I wanted to do at that point, was make the switch from "Done for you," which is what I did with Postfuser, to, "I'll do it with you," or, "How to do it yourself." Break Free Academy was the mechanism for that switch.

I started my own company called Hardcore Closer in that real estate company. I just kept that blog on the back burner, and used it as the way to advertise to loan officers and real estate agents to let us write for them through the Postfuser operation. While I was doing that, I decided I wanted people to learn how to do it themselves, so I launched Break Free Academy. Break Free Academy was a three-day live event that I hosted all by myself. For the event, people came in and learned my modalities. They would set up their own funnels, and leave with leads.

Break Free Academy was 100 percent owned by me. Sean was, at one time, my lead salesperson. He sold the spots to Break Free Academy. We took 8 to 10 on that very first one, for $5000 each. Sean sold the spots, and I would deliver the content for three days. I started Break Free Academy in May of 2013. We had eight people show up at $5,000 apiece. It was a hit.

Immediately, and for the next month, we decided to take it on the road and move from Dallas. We held our second Break Free

Academy in Las Vegas. Las Vegas seemed like a good idea. It's a place everybody can have fun and there's lots of nightlife. Sean, my lead sales guy, also went and helped. But, he and all my clients would go get bottle service every night and wind up completely fucking drunk. That's expected in Vegas and there's nothing wrong with that, however, I stayed in and stayed sober because I had to preach every morning and show everybody how the thing worked. I was lecturing to a bunch of hungover, drunk people. I'm sure it was fine with them, and they probably found it humorous, but at the same time, when someone invests $5,000 in themselves and their business, especially if they've invested that money with me, I want to make sure they get the most out of it.

So, the next time, instead of going to Vegas, we went to Laguna Beach, a more laid back, sleepy city. It's beautiful, with great scenery to take background pictures. We held BFA at a very nice hotel in Laguna Beach And once again, sold 10 spots for $5,000 each. It went well. We took the next month on the road again, this time to Atlantic City, another casino atmosphere. Atlantic City was not a cool place, in my opinion, but we sold 10 spots to that event at $5,000 apiece.

I was tired of going on the road. I started having the same feelings about missing my son that I'd had when I worked at the car dealership. I had to make some moves so I could bring Break Free Academy back to Dallas Texas, and keep it there. That didn't go over so well with Sean. He had also been building a simultaneous business on the side, and it was starting to take off for him as well. We had a falling out. He started making different decisions than me about how he lived, who he surrounded himself with and how he spent money. Not one decision was either right or wrong, but we weren't aligned in the ways we needed to be, so we had to part ways. It wasn't easy. We had struggled for quite a while and gotten in several arguments over money and everything else. I gave him one more chance before we parted ways. We decided to start another company called the Millionaire Masterminds.

I still had my Break Free Academy, and my Hardcore Closer companies that were, and still are, 100 percent owned by me. We decided to launch another, which was OK with me. This time I was willing to partner with somebody else, because my life wasn't 100 percent in the hands of someone else. A. I had ownership and B. I still had two other companies that were my main focus. You'll learn about what those companies did, how we escaped the madness, and the shit that we had to put up with in the next chapter.

Chapter 15

Celebrities

Sean, my business partner, was great at throwing live events and promotions. At the time, Sean sold insurance as a full-time job. He also sold my Break Free Academy spots, and sometimes, my Hardcore Closer spots on the side. He threw these live events as part of the networking group that he'd created. He was a true entrepreneur and a hard worker. It's a sad thing that we both eventually decided to go our separate ways, but before that happened, we started a company called the Million Dollar Masterminds—which later had to be changed to Millionaire Masterminds, thanks to NBC sending us a cease and desist. Sean decided he was going to invite one of the guys from the *Million Dollar Listing* TV show to be a guest at one of the promotion parties he put on for real-estate agents.

The first person we worked with was Josh Flagg out on the West Coast. His grandmother basically brought polyester from Italy to America. She was worth hundreds of millions of dollars. He was the star of the TV show, and was selling multiple million dollar houses. He agreed to come out to the event for five thousand dollars. Sean signed him right there on the spot. We'd pay for his hotel, and he'd come out to the event. Then Josh and I would share the spotlight on the stage. Meanwhile, Sean would be pumping me up, too because he was still selling my stuff. When Josh came out here, we agreed to have him on a radio interview for my *Rockstar Closer Radio* podcast on iTunes. It's still on today, even though I don't add to it anymore. Josh was less than exciting to listen to on the radio. He was a quiet guy, and is very analytical. He wasn't outgoing like he appeared on the show, or at least, he wasn't enthusiastic that day. For all I know, he could have been hungover.

We went to the party that night where Josh was the star and he'd done a great job, and it was a lot of fun. We all hung out. Everybody seemed to like him. He was a lot more personable one-on-one than he'd been on the radio. We were excited. Before he left, Sean offered to start a partnership with Josh, selling spots to a mastermind for $1,000 each. This would be a six-week digital course where Josh would teach people how to sell luxury real estate. You could watch Sean and I make sales to the mastermind on YouTube. I think it's called live sales calls, or something like that. Sean and I ended up selling 30 spots at $1,000 each. Then we paid ourselves evenly three separate ways. At the end of the six weeks, we had an upsell, where we would take people to Beverly Hills. Josh Flagg would show them the impressive houses that he had listed over in Beverly Hills. We sold another 10 spots at $2,500 each to come to Beverly Hills, and hang out with Josh Flagg for the day, and see his listings.

Unfortunately, the day that everybody was to arrive in LAX, there was a shooting. Matter of fact, I came out of Terminal B and five seconds after I came down the stairs, some gentleman decided to go upstairs with a shotgun, and unload on a few people. That meant there were no planes that could land.

That meant nobody could get into LAX. Literally, my flight was the very last one. I didn't even know the shooting had taken place until later during the day when I checked my phone, and saw hundreds of people had messaged me to make sure that I was OK. I found out every single flight of every guest who was come to that event to see Josh Flagg would be delayed as well. Many of them just kept circling in the air for hours waiting on the tower to clear so that they could land. It was a nightmare. I don't know what you think people do when there's nothing to do on an airplane. They surely don't sleep. They drink. These airlines dished out tons of alcohol for free to people for the inconvenience.

When everybody landed, they were, inebriated. That night everybody was supposed to meet Josh for the first time. We had a crew from Detroit that I remember more than any of the others because the dude threw up in his beer mug and he threw up all over the fancy restaurant we were in, too. He threatened Josh Flagg to do a drive-by because he thought he was hitting on his wife. It was a mess. I had to ask them to leave. It was awkward, because these people had just spent a total of $3,500 to be a part of this, including the six-week course, not including the cost of their travel. But it was hard to deal with, because everybody was hungover, drunk and out of control.

Because of that, I wanted to make sure nobody asked for a refund. I had already invested my own money and Sean's money too—into renting the bus to get us around, airline tickets, hotels, setting up Josh, paying him and everything else. We couldn't afford any issues at all. It was an odd bus ride, but I won't get into that. When it was all said and done, everybody had a great time. With this event, we had numbers. We had actual numbers we could take to other guys involved in the Million Dollar Listing TV show, and say, "Hey, we'd like to do this."

We approached Luis, and he wasn't interested. He came, and did a couple of live events, but he didn't want to do a mastermind. We approached Ryan Serhant.

He wasn't interested in doing anything at all. We talked to Fredrik Eklund, who agreed. Fredrik Eklund did a little something different, though. He let me run his social media. Fredrik had 48,000 fans on Facebook when I started. By the time we were done advertising his business, he had over 100,000. I still, today, tell people that when we were in New York, we saw Fredrik's face plastered all over every taxi in the city. I think what drove them to have their best season ever, the one that resulted in an Emmy, was the tens of thousands of dollars we put into his Facebook marketing. I'd venture to wage his Facebook marketing went a lot further, and still does for his brand than anything NBC ever advertised. I'm sure we paid him more money than NBC has ever paid him in all those years as well. I could be wrong, but I don't think so.

We ended up doing the New York thing, and the six-week course with Fredrik just like we'd done with Josh. We sold hundreds of memberships. Fredrik did it 10 times better. Fredrik was awesome to work with. Everybody absolutely loved him, and would fork over money left and right. In total, we wound up doing two tours of $10 million plus penthouses with agents in New York who we charged $2,500 apiece. It was a great time. We'd meet at TAO and have dinner with Fredrik. He's such an entertainer. It was completely awesome.

One day, I think he and Sean had a falling out. Neither one of them really wanted to talk to me about it. I was left in the dark. Then, Fredrik got stuck in an elevator with a bunch of other real estate agents. The elevator was only two floors up, but in that elevator, somebody freaked out and then passed out. He never wanted to be put in that situation again. On top of that, we had to climb eight units which were two stories each with 20-foot ceilings in them, all the way to the very top of the stairs. When we got to the top, we realized we were on the wrong side and had to go all the way down, turn around, and do it all again. Most of the people involved in that trip, were sore and unhappy at the end of the day, Fredrik Eklund included. That would be the last time we'd ever do anything with him.

I still have everything we did with him recorded; it's in a program that if you'd like to look at, I'm happy to show you. It's $497, Just reach out to me.

So, that was it. I was done with business partners. I wouldn't do another damn thing unless it was by my damn self. I'll tell you all about it in the next chapter.

Chapter 16

Riding Solo

I have been dragged through the mud so many times. I have been told how to act and what to do. I have been left with nothing at all except for the clothes on my back because of other people. I'd had all I could take.

While I'd gotten along with the most recent business partners I'd had, I realized there was nobody who was going to keep up with me when it came to doing the work. I realized there was nobody who was going to have the same exact vision as me. If I was going to be able to control my own life and control my own destiny, then I had to step up and do things myself.

I hired a mentor, a gentleman named Kevin Nations. He helped me get clarity on exactly what it was that I wanted. He showed me how I could operate a seven-figure-a-year business by myself. I was excited. I created events. I had been doing the Break Free

Academy before with partners. Now I was leading them by myself. I was ready to take on the world. You can find my mentor here, at Clyxo.com/kevinnations.

I started the Hardcore Closer brand in 2011, and had built it up for a few years, while I'd been blogging the whole time. But I hadn't been doing anything special with it or making programs around it. I guess it was around 2013, when I hired Kevin. Once I started working with him, he helped me map out some of my business. Some of the guys who were in the mastermind helped teach me how to run ads. Within a short period of time, my business started taking off dramatically. I'm talking, seriously escalating.

Once I'd mastered the art of being able to run Facebook ads, I could get in front of millions of people on a weekly basis within a short period of time…just by throwing money behind it. During that time, the haters arrived. I'd stood out on my own. I was tattooed up. I didn't wear suits. I told it like it is. I had a lot of sales under my belt.

I still have a lot of sales under my belt. I still complete and close sales every single day. People would tell me, "Stop cussing. You're never going to make it in this business. You can't tell people that you've been to prison. You can't tell people to fuck off when they argue with you on your deals. You're supposed to accept trolls. You're just supposed to be there as a person to give us motivation." All these people consistently told me I wasn't going to be around. Guess what? I didn't listen to those people. I was riding solo, and nobody could tell me shit. Nobody could take my money. The people who told me to stop cussing were never going to fucking pay me a dime anyway. Being a salesman and having thick skin, I wasn't scared to listen to what the trolls said. After about six months of running ads and being in their face, time and time again, they shut the fuck up.

I remember when Facebook ads were first coming on the scene. I was one of the first people to start advertising in a major way on Facebook in 2013. People would say things like, "Get out of my newsfeed, you fucking salesman. Get out of my newsfeed! I don't want to read your shit." I went through every bit of trolling imaginable. It used to make me mad. I would get emails from people who hated me. I used to comment back and forth and argue with people. I've had to block people on Facebook because of it. Then one day, I just let my assistant start taking my emails. I let my assistant start dealing with the Facebook page. I would post and then I would never check it again. You know why? Because I didn't want to let small minds deteriorate my big goal. I didn't want people who weren't closing sales to get in the way of the people who were closing sales.

After a while of staying the course while telling the truth, fucking cussing, and just being me the weak salespeople went away. I attracted a herd of only Alpha salespeople, both males and females. I started working with the perfect clients. Meanwhile, all the pussies, the people who were telling me how to live my life according to the bullshit rules they were using to live their lives, started disappearing. That was when I first realized I was becoming bulletproof.

Short of just doing something absolutely asinine, I could say anything I wanted. I could do anything I wanted. I could be selective. I could tell people, "Fuck you. Here's your money. Take it back." I could tell people, "Hey, I'll help provide for your family and for the rest of the freaking legacy you plan on leaving." I could handle things my way. I was in total control. No gunfire, no bullet shot my way could stop the brand I was going to build by my damn self.

Chapter 17

The REAL Ryan Stewman

You know, being bulletproof didn't just happen overnight. It took months and years honestly, of running Facebook ads. At this point, in 2016, I've been running Facebook ads every single day consistently for three years. I've spent hundreds of thousands of dollars on that ad platform and hundreds of thousands of dollars on many other ad platforms. I didn't grow to have the 50,000 fans I have at this moment and the 50,000 people I have on my subscriber list with one fancy email or one fancy blog post. It took me posting three times a week trying to get people's attention, figuring out which ones worked the best and boosting those—as well as figuring out which ones didn't—and deleting them. It took me getting into groups and having a thick skin as a salesman to be able to say what was on my mind. That didn't happen overnight.

In 2014, I was getting tired of being berated by trolls on Facebook. I was going through a family situation, and my wife at the time and I weren't getting along. We weren't on the same page together. I was blowing money left and right, and it was making her nervous, and for all the right reasons. But I was still pretending to be this person who was reserved. I wasn't the real Ryan Stewman. I hadn't emerged as the person you see who's written this book. I hadn't told my story yet. Nobody really knew I had been to prison. Nobody knew I used to sell drugs. Nobody knew any of that stuff. As bulletproof as I was at that moment, there were still people behind the scenes who were going to throw smoke bombs my way if I didn't go ahead and make all that stuff public and address it upfront.

The mentor I hired was a gentleman named Garrett J. White with the *Wake Up Warrior* program. I was warrior number 15 when I started. I stuck with Garrett as a mentor for a year. Garrett liberated me. He helped me break the shell and prove to the world who I really am. He helped me not give a fuck about the haters and start giving love to the lovers. I would never forget when I went on his radio show. Garrett introduced me and took a breath, and he must have just hit the mute button on his microphone. I told my whole story about being adopted, going to prison, getting divorced and everything else. I told it all, the dying, hookers, drugs; I left nothing out. He was blown away. The audience loved it. To this day, it's his most popular podcast.

At the same time, that wasn't the lifestyle my wife wanted me talking about. It would only be a matter of time before the real Ryan Stewman would have to emerge from that relationship, like many others. At this point in my life, my parents weren't happy with my telling this story either. I had to end those relationships. As hard as they were to end, they were relationships holding me back. I couldn't go to the next level carrying dead weight that would be happy at my present level. When your vision is bigger than the vision of the people around you, you must make bold moves. A lot of people can't track with somebody who's making bold moves. Just like in the past, I'd had to get rid of business partners. I knew that if I was going to become completely bulletproof, I was going to have to get rid of more than just business partners. I was going to have to get rid of every tie holding me down, no matter how hard it was to break those ties. It's still hard today.

I didn't earn the moniker Hardcore Closer for nothing. I didn't get to where I am by taking the easy road. I didn't build a bulletproof business by being a fucking pussy and trying to cater to everybody's needs. I had to build a business based around customers and a family of choice. I chose to be with the woman I'm with right now. I've chosen to take her son under my wing. I've chosen to be the best dad that I can for Jax and spend as much time with him as humanly possible. That meant I also had to choose to end some other relationships on the way.

There's one thing that I've noticed by building this bulletproof lifestyle and business. Along the way, you're going to drop things off. You're going to lose relationships. You're going to lose business partners. You might even lose family members when you go to the extreme like I have. At the same time, you'll always gain more, because when you give up the dead weight, what you have in the other hand is a hot air balloon that allows you to ascend. You see, when you stop and throw away the sandbags, the hot air moves the balloon a lot higher and at a lot faster pace. That's what you have to do sometimes and oftentimes, these are hard decisions to make, but they're the ones that need to be made. We can allow ourselves to get held in the same place. We can be advised not to cuss and not to tell our story, but at the same time, how big of an asshole would I be if I didn't tell my story? How big of a dick move would it be if I hadn't gotten in front of the public and said, "I'm broken, just like you. Here's how I'm healing"?

What if I didn't share my story? What if I didn't share the methods that have allowed me to cope and grow the thick skin I have? What if I hadn't done any of that stuff? It would be selfish of me, like it was selfish of those who were sandbagging me and asking me to keep quiet. I knew if I was going to do this, I was going to have to do it myself. I was going to have to be the real Ryan Stewman, and I was going to have to do what I do best, and that's keep it real. I'm proud to say that still, at this point, that is exactly the mission I'm on. I have not been deterred. I have not been thrown off track. I am still dead on these tracks running full steam ahead. Along the way, I've had a lot of obstacles come up, too. You're about to learn some of those lessons in the next chapters.

Chapter 18

Lawyer Up

Here's the deal. When I was getting rid of some of those relationships in my life, I realized that you had to have everything on paper. I had to lawyer up when I was going through the divorce. My lawyer evaluated my business and came back to me. He said, "Good news, your business is worth nothing." That was a shock to me, because I'd built this whole bulletproof, unstoppable machine that was just rolling full steam ahead. To be told it was absolutely worthless was a jaw-dropping moment for me. The lawyer would go on to explain that not only was my business worthless, but if I got into some sort of medical trouble, if I had an accident, or if I was killed, then my business would be absolutely valueless. Nobody would continue to pay me for consulting services if I was no longer around to consult.

It was one of those, "Come to Jesus," moments for me, because I had created this whole lifestyle business around the things Kevin Nations had taught me. These things had served me well and made me a lot of money, but he was right. If I went away, there was no legacy left. There was no money for my son, Jax. There was no money for me to take care of Amy and Asher. All that would be gone. I started asking my lawyer for business advice, "What do you recommend doing?" He had absolutely zero words of wisdom for me, like most attorneys, so I ended up hiring a CEO for my company.

The CEO, Jim Friel, stuck around for about 90 days, which was his contract time period, and he set me up to where I could scale my business, have a sales team and sell digital products. I'd had these digital products forever, but I was always trying to push big ticket sales, which was the Kevin Nations' model. The big-ticket sales are awesome, but I never thought about pushing my lower ticket, digital products to prospects when they said they couldn't afford it. Jim saw that hole in my business, pointed it out and showed me where there was a way to profit and handle things in a different manner. Whether he even realized he'd done that or not, it made me understand some new possibilities were available to me. From there, I figured, "OK, I have these digital assets I can sell. They're actually worth something." That's what I started pushing.

In 2015, I pushed as hard as I could, to sell as many digital products as possible. It was a very liberating experience because, once I'd delivered a sale on a digital product, it was as easy as giving somebody a login and a password. I didn't have to spend any time with them. It was the most time-efficient way possible for me to sell. None of my programs were recurring revenue models, but they went anywhere from $27 to $1,497, and were digital products I could close on sales calls, all day, every day. I was averaging about 50 sales a month, and about three months into it getting burnt out real quick. So, I decided to scale my business and started hiring a team. Out of the woodwork, everybody showed up wanting a job. These people thought they could be a part of the Hardcore Closer organization, but it wasn't as easy as they thought. I had to go through a lot of dead weight.

I realized that selling these digital products enabled me to profit from an area of my business that had just been sitting there and not making me money. That allowed me to hire the best CPA firm in the nation to structure my business and to handle my taxes: Stoner Albright. They've been able to put me together better than anybody I've ever had, and I've hired bunches of CPAs in the past. They've allowed me to hire some of the best intellects and business attorneys and keep them on retainers.

Now that I've built this huge business, I want to continue to make it bulletproof. Once you have contractors selling for you, they make mistakes. Once you have a sales team in place, they make mistakes. An Operations Manager will make mistakes. If you cuss online, you put a target on your back. If you start making a lot of money, you put a target on your back. For me to continue running my company as a bulletproof business, I had to lawyer up. At this point in my career, I haven't been sued for my company. We handle everything with the utmost composure and service, and deal with it all. We've never been put on the "Ripoff Report." We've never even had dissatisfied customers, except for times when I have personally had to give money back, when I've told someone to kick rocks.

While I've been building my business, I am fully aware that at any moment I could be under attack and shots could be fired again. But, because of my experiences, I know to lawyer up and explain to the lawyer what's happened to me in the past. Also because of past experiences, I know to get the right CPA, because this thing's going to take off and I'm going to need it structured properly. It's been a liberating experience as I've said. As much as I don't like dealing with lawyers and CPAs, the ones I've surrounded myself with, Lorne Book and Gene Stoner, have put another pane of bulletproof glass in my machine and in this business which shows no signs of slowing its momentum for the foreseeable future.

Chapter 19

Hiring Talent (Not Partners)

I had the CPA, I had the lawyer and I had the digital products, but I was getting burned out. Like I'd mentioned in the previous chapter, I had decided it was time to start hiring a sales team. Instead of having employees and needing to deal with taxes and everything else, I assembled a team of affiliates who agreed to take leads in exchange for commissions on each one of their sales.

I would make some offers in my Sales Talk With Sales Pro group on Facebook, which consisted of about 10,000 members at the time. Everybody and their mother came out of the woodwork wanting a job. I know from past experiences that if a vision doesn't align with me, I have to cut ties quick. I would give people chances. People would spend days, weeks and months persuading me to give them a chance. I'd send them over a few leads, and they'd fall off the map. I wasn't necessarily looking for the best salesperson, because I can train a person to become a Closer. I wasn't necessarily looking for the smoothest-talking devil in the group. I was just looking for someone who was willing to put in the work.

It took me hiring and firing 20, 30, 40 different affiliate salespeople, to where I was exhausted. In one month, I had let everybody go and decided to do it myself. Then I realized I was even more exhausted. So, I started hiring again. It's been an uphill battle to find talent. I realized, through searching for all this talent, you have to just find hard workers. Whether they're good salesmen or have good sales skills or not, if you find somebody who's willing to do the work and you have enough leads to get them in front of enough people, they'll make sales.

If they're willing to do the work, that means they're willing to do the follow up. If they're willing to do the follow up, it means they'll make sales.

If they're willing to do the work, it means they're willing to take the training. If they're willing to take the training, they're willing to learn and implement and it all goes back to the fact that it's because they're willing to do the work. Which means that they'll make more money.

I found hard workers. I put them in charge of a product that best fit their situation. For example, if I have somebody who comes from the car business, a $200 payment is not much for them to ask. It's comfortable. It's in their zone. If I have somebody from the real estate world who's one of my affiliates, a $1,500 payment is comfortable to them because it's in their zone. I place my team accordingly.

When I was going through all this hiring and firing, there was one thing I didn't want to do. I didn't want to give a bunch of free sales training out to people. I didn't want guys to come on to my program, think they were going to be able to work with me one-on-one, get my time and learn sales and then go somewhere else. I knew a lot of the intention of the marketplace was to work for me to get free sales training and possibly get paid at the same time. I'm smarter than that. I built a bulletproof business. Instead, I had the new people log into my sales training program, Show Up and Close, which you can check out at buyshowupandclose.com. If you go to buyshowupandclose.com, you'll see my $500 sales training. I make every one of our affiliates buy that program first and go through the sales training. I will not speak to them and I will not work with them until they've made 10 sales. I don't care if it's $27 or $27,000. They're required to make 10 sales before they're given any face time or any phone time to ask me questions. That's understood going in. Not only have they bought the product they're selling, they're learning my methods. They're willing to do the work. It doesn't take any of my time until they have made me money, but they start making me money the second they show up because they've immediately purchased one of my programs.

This is how I've been able to attract players. This is how I've been able to run my entire business and hire and fire so many people without wasting massive amounts of my time. If you are a manager or if you are a business owner, you should record every single move you make when you train a new person, and put it all on video. That way, when you've got the whole, complete video series done, all you've got to do is turn around and when the next new person comes on, you tell them, "Watch these videos. If you have any questions after each video, feel free to reach out to me," or, "Watch these videos. Don't come talk to me until you've watched every one and made 10 sales,"—if you want to follow my model.

It works. It saves you time. One of the biggest time wasters we have in our business, which allows us to be vulnerable and not bulletproof, is that we're stuck doing things that don't make us money. Training salespeople does not make you money. Sure, a salesperson being trained and being able to make sales makes you money but, while you're training them, it is not making you money. It is taking your time away from somewhere else that could be making you money. Instead, record all your stuff, put it in front of the next person you hire, save the time and continue to make money. That's how a bulletproof business is run, and that's how I run mine. Talent is so hard to find. If you spend your time with the wrong people, it's like owning stock, watching the stock decline, but not selling it because you're attached to the stock. You love the stock. You bought the stock when it was at X price. Even though your stockbroker's telling you, "Sell, motherfucker, sell!" you're still trying to hold onto it because to you it has some sort of sentimental value. I feel the same way about salespeople. Salespeople are commodities. Everybody and their mother is a salesperson. It's not hard to find salespeople. What's hard is to find a person who will work their ass off. If you find a person who will work their ass off, you can turn them into a salesperson. You can do that with automation if you'll just follow my lead, and record the information that you need to use in order to train people.

Chapter 20

Rubber Bullets

The year is 2015. I'm business-partner free. I'm divorced. I'm all by myself ready to do whatever it takes to step up. I set my goal to reach a million people a month. Whether through my blog, Facebook, or another social media outlet. I wanted to reach a million people a month. I knew I was going to have to make some bold moves, because I was reaching about 3,000 people a month at the time. It was a big goal. It was a goal I never thought I could achieve. I was willing to do the work. As I've said in the previous chapter, if you will just find somebody who will outwork everybody else, it will be hard for people to keep up. I'll take somebody who works hard over talent any day of the week, just because I know myself as a hard worker. I can always rely on someone willing to do the work. That's exactly what I did. I did the work. I doubled down on my advertisements.

People talked more and more shit to me, but I was making giant revenue. I was making more money than I've ever made before. I still continue to. At one point, about mid-2015, I think it was June or July, I hit my first cash money, six-figure month. That meant I had collected over $100,000 in gross sales in one single 31-day period. I was excited, because that had been my goal for years and I had come close—50 and 60 grand—but I had never reached that six-figure-in- a-month thing. Once I'd had that victory, I realized I could also be in front of 1.6 million people that month. Then I got the direct correlation. A million-people meant six figures in income for the month.

I ramped it up.

I met some guys who worked for Hewlett-Packard, supposedly the best website guys in the business and I paid them $25,000 to set up a website that could handle the traffic. They moved me over to servers and gave me a more familiar look. They had a design team meet at my house three times. It was an experience I'll never forget. These guys were the nerdiest of Internet nerds that you could possibly imagine, but they were super intelligent when it came to this stuff. They love numbers. They were just number crunching, SEO website guys, who work for Fortune 500 companies. I still employ these guys today. They're actually general contractors who do all of my SEO and website work. They are brilliant. I can't thank Corey Hubble enough. Because of a $25,000 investment into that website, our traffic in the month of June went from 3,000 views a month to 30,000. We had 10x the views on our blog within 30 days! The next month, it was 50,000. The next month, 100,000; people were coming to our blog. By September of 2015, we were having regular months of 200,000+ visits and unique hits to my blog...in a single month. We were hitting a million to 1.5 million people each and every single week and continue to do so today.

With more exposure comes more vulnerability. When you're getting big in front of an audience like that, the haters stack up and come in droves. The trolls and the know-it-alls come out. The shots were fired again, but this time they might as well have been rubber bullets, because of my bulletproof vest. Because of the way I'd built my entire business, it didn't matter. Those who say, "I'm not going to buy from you because you cuss," well, they no longer matter, because they weren't going to buy in the first place. At the same time, I had built a community of 10,000 people in my sales group and 50,000 people on my Facebook page. I had raving fans and customers all over the place and still do. Anytime somebody talks shit now, the fans diminish them. They make them irrelevant and show their paycheck stubs. They show the results of the leads they're getting. It's an amazing thing.

Growing a business from zero to one million was a lot of hard work. It took me several years before I hit the million-dollar mark in my business. I'm not talking a million dollars in 12 months. I'm just talking about a million dollars earned. About three years' time is what I needed. I know you hear a lot of people brag about building an overnight success, but a lot of those people blow up, and here's why. They don't have a bulletproof business. They may have made a million dollars overnight, but when shots are fired at them, they spend that million dollars fighting. They are just like a lottery winner; easy come, easy go. Overnight sensations are just that, gone in the next day. I wanted to build a business that was sustainable and a brand that would last a long time. I wanted to build a brand that could keep going, even if I died.

Since I've scaled my sales team, I now have coaches on staff. My coaches live by the same bulletproof code. They're unstoppable. They tell it like it is. People hire us because they want to hear it like it is, for the same reason I hired Kevin Nations and Garrett J. White. People want to hear the truth. In a world full of lies and fakeness, having someone tell you how it really works and someone who can give you the inside experience from the experiments that they've done can change the game for you. That's now what the Hardcore Closer brand is doing for millions upon millions of people on a monthly basis.

It's because I made the investments and surrounded myself with the right people. Now, when the rubber bullets are fired, they can't stop this seven-figure machine. In three years, we've gone from zero to one million, to now doing more than a million dollars every 12 months. Six-figure months in revenue are expected, not exciting. As a matter of fact, multiple six-figures-per-month revenue is expected in this organization. My monthly Amex bills are more than the national median income in the richest country in the world. It's a surreal feeling to know I've come all the way from the penitentiary to a penthouse, ironically, surrounded by bulletproof glass.

I'll tell you where we go from here in the next couple of chapters, and some things you can do to bulletproof your own business.

Chapter 21

When the Smoke Clears

One thing about building a bulletproof business is that it's not just your business that becomes bulletproof. If people say something to me on the streets, it doesn't faze me. If people say something to me in an email, it doesn't faze me, because they don't know how hard I've worked. They don't know the work I've put into designing this business. Alongside designing it, I wanted to make sure I didn't lose relationships again, so I've had to build balance this time. I learned about building balance from Kevin Nations, like the "Four Fs", or what Garrett J. White calls his "Core Four." Those things have changed my direction and vision.

Once I got clear on what it is that I wanted in my business, Garrett said one of the most brilliant things I've ever heard, "You're super clear on what you want in your business. Are you super clear on what you want in your life?" I wasn't. When the smoke cleared, I realized I wasn't clear on what kind of a spouse or companion I wanted, or what kind of lifestyle I wanted to leave for my kids. I was just doing this business thing and letting everything else fall into place. Once again, I had been left vulnerable. I was not vulnerable on the business side, but I was vulnerable on the balance side with my family. As I've mentioned in previous chapters, I don't speak with my parents or grandparents, or really any blood members of my family anymore. It's unfortunate, but those were ties I had to cut. Jackson, my son, was all I had. But later on, in 2014, Amy and Asher made their way into my life. By design, Amy was exactly who I got clear about, thanks to Garrett J. White. She was a salesperson and a mother, energy-driven, with a great job. She was everything I wanted, and still is. I had to make the time to build this bulletproof business, but I also had to make time to be with the people I love, the people I had been waiting my entire life to embrace. These were the people I wanted to spend my life with; Jackson, Amy and Asher. I had to get rigorous about a schedule, because I'd lost three marriages before.

I only had partial custody of my son because of my rigorous schedule. I was going to make damn sure that I did everything different this time concerning balance as well. I started to schedule. I'd always scheduled my entire business, but I'd never scheduled my home life. I started running everything on a schedule. Amy and I go out on date nights once a week. We put it on our calendar. We know that that night is our night together. That time has been reserved for us. When my kids want to go to the park or they want to go to the jump house, or they want to do any of that, they put it on my schedule, because they know that that time is reserved for them. They look at my calendar and they see the end of the day, and they say, "Dad, your schedule is open. We can go," and they put it on the calendar. I made time for business all these years, and destroyed relationships, marriages and everything else, because I didn't put time on my calendar. The calendar was reserved for business. I lived and died by the calendar—

but today the calendar is reserved for everybody—my friends, my family, and my business.

I have to understand if I'm vulnerable on one side, if I'm fighting with Amy at home, then that makes me vulnerable in my business. I can't have a bulletproof business unless I've got my family bulletproofed as well. Why would I want to have a bulletproof business if I couldn't bulletproof my family as well?

Following the same exact steps to protect them with lawyers, trust, wills, insurance and every other precaution I'd taken for my business, I've also now taken for my family. I have built a bulletproof everything. Because when the shots are fired and the smoke clears, I want my family to still be standing there. I want my business to still be standing tall. When you watch old Discovery Channel documentaries and see the war-torn buildings in some of these Third World countries, there's always that one building, usually a government building, sitting there untouched. That's my business.

Not only is it bulletproof, it's bomb-proof. The good thing is, I have bomb-proofed my personal life as well.

If nothing's bothering me and I'm not vulnerable and I'm not penetrable in my family life, then nobody can mess with me or penetrate anything I've got going on in my business life. I've created a balance that's unstoppable. As a Libra, I can say that's something I've tried my whole life to accomplish, but it's not always been something I thought was possible until I decided to bulletproof everything.

Chapter 22

Building Your Own Bulletproof Business

The idea behind this entire book was for me to be able to share my experiences through stories and things that I've gone through, including the hardships that I've had to struggle with to get where I am today. It's also to open your eyes to all the pitfalls that happen in business. These pitfalls may include the partners who unexpectedly stop working, who bolt on you, take your money, or have different visions. They may be family members or a spouse who sometimes doesn't have the same dream or vision as you. To help you avoid the roller coaster months, I wanted these experiences that I've had and all these shenanigans that I've endured to empower you. That way, when you see one of these opportunities, or one of these bullets fired at you in the future, you'll be able to keep your vest on and deflect them as well.

Oftentimes, if we become apologetic, and we let the crowd dictate how we act in front of them, they'll hold it against you. You see, whether it be in business, or real life, two fake entities will entertain each other for a lifetime as long as one of them doesn't ever call the other fake. It's like an unspoken agreement. I'm fake; you're fake. We can pretend to be fake together, and nobody will know that we're fake except for each other. If one of you breaks that agreement, one of you becomes vulnerable and it changes the game. If you're going to build a bulletproof business, you're going to have to break away the fake agreements you have with your friends and family. They have got to end. That mindset must go away. You can't make a million dollars a year thinking like a six-figure person. You can't make a billion dollars with a seven-figure mentality. When I was only earning $100,000 a year, I focused on earning a million. I thought like a millionaire. Now that I earn a million dollars a year, I think like a billionaire, because that's the next step for me.

Here's the thing, if you're going to go to the top, you're going to need to be tough. Nobody fought their way to being king of the hill without getting scars or without bruises. They say salesmen should have thick skin. We do, because enough people are going to tell us, "no" or to fuck off. We've got to be able to take that and not be emotionally invested every time it happens.

If you're going to build a bulletproof business, you're going to have to do the same thing. You're going to have to uncover all your dirt and make sure nobody can hold it against you. You're going to have to lawyer up. You're going to have to hire the best CPAs. If you want to build a seven-figure business, you don't want a shitty lawyer on your staff. You don't want a shitty CPA on your staff. When things go wrong, those are the first people to get the blame. If they suck, and they know that you know they suck, who the fuck is to blame in the first place? In reality, it's just you.

I'd like to encourage you to follow me on social media through clyxo.com/closer. Just pick out your favorite social media channel and follow me there. While you're at it, make sure you sign up for Clyxo—it's another one of my bulletproof businesses.

If you enjoyed this book, if you took a few lessons from it, if you learned a few things to keep you from bumping your head against the wall, share this with a friend. Share it with another salesperson or a fellow entrepreneur who needs to read about these lessons. Share it with somebody who you care about to help them avoid some of the pitfalls and backtrack I've had to go through. The whole idea behind this book is to help people avoid some of the mistakes I've made in my career. If you know somebody who's doing entrepreneurial work right now, someone who is starting their own business, this book needs to find its way into their hands. Just as the experiences and the lessons learned in this book have helped to open your eyes, you owe it to the person who you know you could help—to open their eyes.

I've gone from zero dollars and living in the basement of my ex in-laws' house, to the penthouse. You can do it as well. Maybe you don't have to get as outrageous and go as far left and right as I did. If you'll just find yourself, be yourself, you'll find what they call your inner peace. You'll be unstoppable. Lastly, it would be weird to write this whole book without telling you that if you're looking for someone to consult you, guide you and mentor you through the process of building a bulletproof business, I'm your guy. Look, I don't work with pussies. I don't work with excuse makers. I don't work with non-action takers. It's not inexpensive to work with me, but I'm worth every single penny x100 that I charge. If you'd like to know more about working with me, just go to hardcorecloser.com.

Find a way to get an application over to me. Mention in the application that you read this book, and your application will come personally to my desk. We'll have a serious sales conversation about what the investment on your end will be and how I can help you to grow your business and make it bulletproof so it's the best it can be.

Thank you for reading.